UNITED WE STAND

★

UNITED WE STAND

Flying the American Flag

★

Peter Gwillim Kreitler

CHRONICLE BOOKS

SAN FRANCISCO

Acknowledgments

I would like to thank my friends Marguerite Storm, who saved many covers during the summer of 1942, and her daughter Mrs. Grant (Jacquette) Theis, who donated them to the Thrift Shop of St. Matthew's Church in Pacific Palisades, California; and Mary Muller, its director, who told me of their existence and who enabled me to acquire them. I would also like to thank peditiatrician Dr. Tom Santuli, researcher; Bart Bartholomew, photographer; Bob Kline, patriot; and Maureen and Eric Lasher, literary agents, for their help in developing this book. A special thanks to my wife, Katy, whose support and patience with me has been exemplary. A final thanks to the countless individuals across America who have saved these icons of our history so that they could be assembled for all to see forever.

This book is dedicated to the generation of women, men, boys, and girls of the United States who witnessed and were inspired by these magazines when they were first published. It is also dedicated to the patriotic women and men of these times who serve our country in many ways, so that the freedoms we all enjoy are preserved.

Text and compilation copyright © 2001 by Peter Gwillim Kreitler. Individual covers copyright by the respective magazines. All rights reserved. No part of this book may be reproduced in any form without written permission from the publisher.

A special tribute to the staff at the National Museum of American History, especially Marilyn Zoidis, Helena Wright, and Katy Kendrick, who have worked hard to bring the *United We Stand* exhibition to fruition.

Cover illustration from *True Story* magazine. Photograph on page 7 reproduced from the Farm Security Administration Collection of the Library of Congress.

The magazine covers are part of the Katy and Peter Kreitler Collection.

Library of Congress Cataloging-in-Publication Data available.

ISBN: 0-8118-3521-9

Designed by Vivien Sung
Printed in the United States of America

Distributed in Canada by Raincoast Books
9050 Shaughnessy Street
Vancouver, British Columbia V6P 6E5

10 9 8 7 6 5 4 3 2 1

Chronicle Books LLC
85 Second Street
San Francisco, California 94105

www.chroniclebooks.com

Introduction

Following the bombing of Pearl Harbor on December 7, 1941, magazines across the United States joined in an unprecedented campaign to inspire the country: for the Fourth of July, 1942, each magazine would feature the American flag on its cover.

Nearly three hundred magazines took part in the United We Stand campaign and published dramatic images of Old Glory, announcing from every street corner and news rack that the nation was together and ready for the challenges ahead.

The idea for concerted action by magazines came from Paul MacNamara, a publicist for Hearst magazines. He believed it would allow magazines both to show their patriotism and to sell more copies, while raising the public's awareness of the magazine industry. The promotion was supported by the National Publishers Association and by the newly formed United States Flag Association, as well as by Secretary of the Treasury Henry M. Morgenthau Jr., who urged the publishers to also use the Buy War Bonds and Stamps insignia on their covers.

The design of the cover and the treatment of the flag were left to the magazines, and the range of cover imagery was as varied as the magazines themselves. The *Family Circle* portrays a mother, father, and their two children waving flags as a pair of soldiers march past. *House Beautiful* features a Norman Rockwellesque home flying the flag from its front-yard flagpole. *Successful Farming* adds the flag to a typical domestic farm scene. *Gourmet* features a crossed-flag motif behind trays of desserts. *Metals and Alloys* shows Old Glory in the foreground of an array of industrial machinery, perhaps in production of U.S. tanks. The *Rudder,* "the magazine for yachtsmen," features the flag flying from the stern of a boat on an open sea.

In an image that speaks of the nation's commitment at all levels of society to winning the war, the *Poultry Tribune* features a lad of about seven, wearing a homemade paper military cap, standing at attention and saluting. On the table in front of him, rows of eggs in platoon formation carry miniature rifles, while the leading egg carries a tiny American flag. *Superman, Dick Tracy,* and other comics joined in, with Captain Marvel Jr. swinging from the Liberty Bell on the cover of *Master Comics* and Donald Duck marching with Pluto in *Walt Disney's Comics. Ace Comics* placed the first verse of "America" on its front cover as well.

In addition to depicting the flag, approximately half of the magazines included the words "United We Stand" on their covers, spelling out the campaign theme and reminding citizens that a unified nation was key to success on distant battlefields. Several magazines continued to publish patriotic covers in subsequent years, and of course, many of the magazines also published patriotic sentiments inside.

The focus of this book is on the covers of the July campaign, though a few other covers from 1942 are included. That was also the year that Congress officially recognized the Pledge of Allegiance, which had been written in 1892 by Francis Bellamy, the circulation manager of the *Youth's Companion* magazine. The Pledge as it was worded in 1942 (the words "under God" were added in 1954) is reproduced in this book, along with other songs and expressions of pride for the flag.

LIFE

DECEMBER 22, 1941 **10** CENTS
YEARLY S

LIFE

UNITED WE STAND

JULY 6, 1942 **10** CENTS
YEARLY SUBSCRIPTION $4.50

Two covers, published seven months apart, capture the national mood and the significance of the campaign to the American spirit. Two weeks after the bombing of Pearl Harbor in December 1941, *Life* magazine published a stark, black-and-white image of the flag, reflecting the low national morale of the time. The July 6, 1942, cover of the magazine again features the flag, but now in bold full color, flying with confidence. Newsstands filled with flags beaming from the covers of dozens and dozens of publications sent a vibrant and vital message, reinforced by cover displays at over twelve hundred leading department stores. In July 1942, the greatest symbol of our nation's unity was everywhere.

This book, published in conjunction with the *United We Stand* exhibition at the National Museum of American History, Smithsonian Institution, pays tribute to an almost-forgotten campaign by American magazines, and to the men and women behind them. It also salutes the citizens who stood together in support of their country, and reveals the spirit of a special time in American history, a patriotic zeal and pride still inspiring today.

VOGUE

"United We Stand"

ADVANCE
RETAIL
TRADE
EDITION

See section facing page 74

JULY 1, 1942 · PRICE 35 CENTS
40 CENTS IN CANADA

BUY WAR BONDS
AND STAMPS
FOR VICTORY

CORONET

JULY   25c

"United We Stand"

Complete 15,000 word authentic life story of

GENERAL DOUGLAS MacARTHUR

including an original life portrait in full color!

AUGUST **REDBOOK** 25 CENTS
M A G A Z I N E

"UNITED WE STAND"

Beginning a New Serial by **MARGARET AYER BARNES**

New Claudia
BY ROSE FRANKEN **BY BEN HECHT**

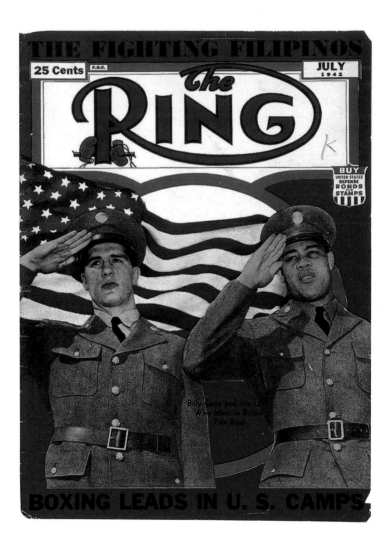

I pledge allegiance to my Flag
and the Republic for which it stands,
one nation indivisible,
with liberty and justice for all.

★

"THE PLEDGE OF ALLEGIANCE"

Francis Bellamy

THE SATURDAY EVENING

POST

JULY 4, 1942
VOLUME 215. NUMBER 1

10¢

UNITED WE STAND

EDGAR SNOW REPORTS FROM CALCUTTA

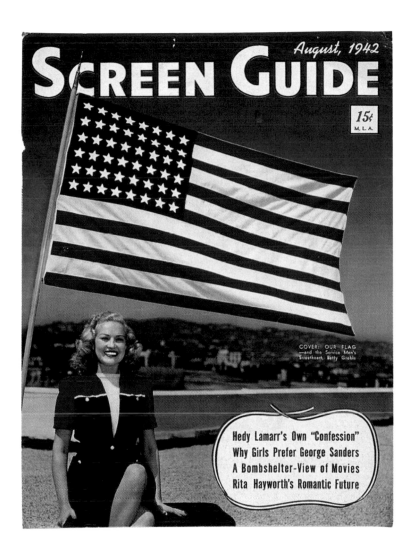

August, 1942

SCREEN GUIDE

15¢
M. L. A.

COVER: OUR FLAG
—and the Service Men's
Sweetheart, Betty Grable

Hedy Lamarr's Own "Confession"
Why Girls Prefer George Sanders
A Bombshelter-View of Movies
Rita Hayworth's Romantic Future

PHOTOPLAY
LARGEST CIRCULATION OF ANY SCREEN MAGAZINE
combined with
MOVIE MIRROR
10¢
AUGUST
"UNITED WE STAND"
PHOTOGRAPH BY PAUL HESSE
IN THE SERVICE
TWO GREAT MAGAZINES FOR THE PRICE OF ONE
HOW CLARK GABLE IS CONQUERING LONELINESS

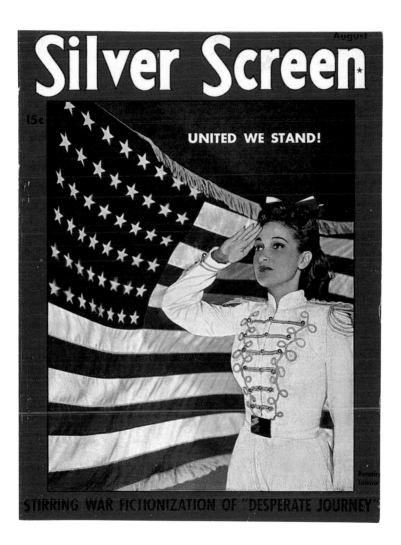

MOVIE-RADIO
GUIDE

FIFTEEN CENTS

PROGRAMS FOR JULY 4—10

UNITED WE STAND

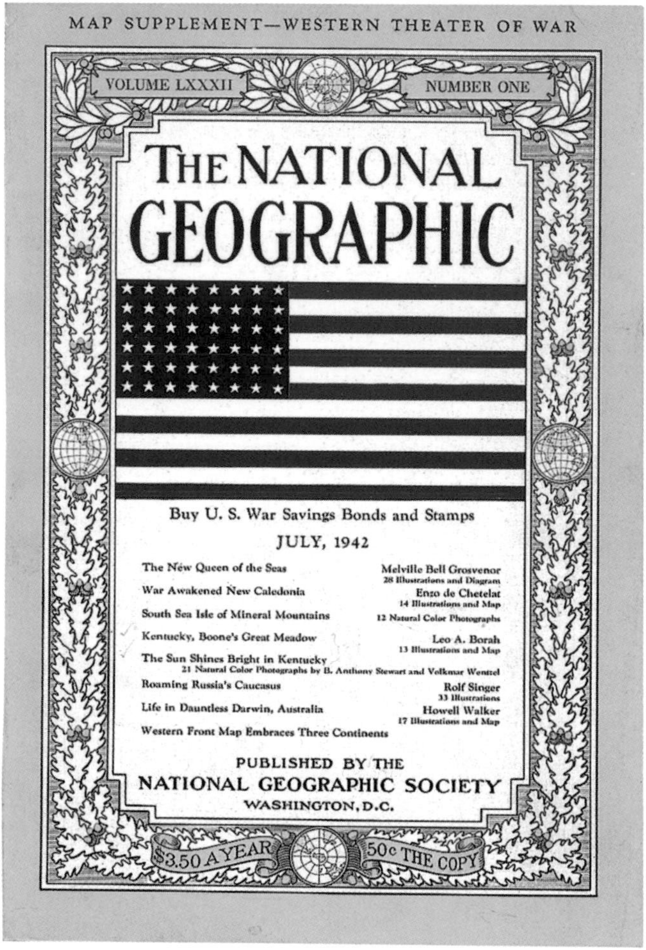

MAP SUPPLEMENT—WESTERN THEATER OF WAR
VOLUME LXXXII
NUMBER ONE
THE NATIONAL GEOGRAPHIC
Buy U. S. War Savings Bonds and Stamps
JULY, 1942
The New Queen of the Seas
Melville Bell Grosvenor
28 Illustrations and Diagram
War Awakened New Caledonia
Enzo de Chetelat
14 Illustrations and Map
South Sea Isle of Mineral Mountains
12 Natural Color Photographs
Kentucky, Boone's Great Meadow
Leo A. Borah
13 Illustrations and Map
The Sun Shines Bright in Kentucky
21 Natural Color Photographs by B. Anthony Stewart and Volkmar Wentzel
Roaming Russia's Caucasus
Rolf Singer
33 Illustrations
Life in Dauntless Darwin, Australia
Howell Walker
17 Illustrations and Map
Western Front Map Embraces Three Continents
PUBLISHED BY THE
NATIONAL GEOGRAPHIC SOCIETY
WASHINGTON, D.C.
$3.50 A YEAR
50c THE COPY

SPECIAL ISSUE ON MORALE

The Saturday Review
of Literature

Vol. XXV No. 27 | New York, Saturday, July 4, 1942 | Fifteen Cents

Articles and Reviews by:

ELEANOR ROOSEVELT
Editor

GEORGE V. DENNY, Jr.

HOUSTON PETERSON
Associate Guest Editors

WILLIAM ROSE BENÉT

RUTH BENEDICT

NORMAN CORWIN

VIRGINIUS DABNEY

LIEUT. COL. JOSEPH I. GREENE

HANS KOHN

CARROLL C. PRATT

JAMES RESTON

CHARLES J. ROLO

ROGER SHAW

GEORGE N. SHUSTER

LAURA POLANYI STRIKER

ORDWAY TEAD

UNITED WE STAND

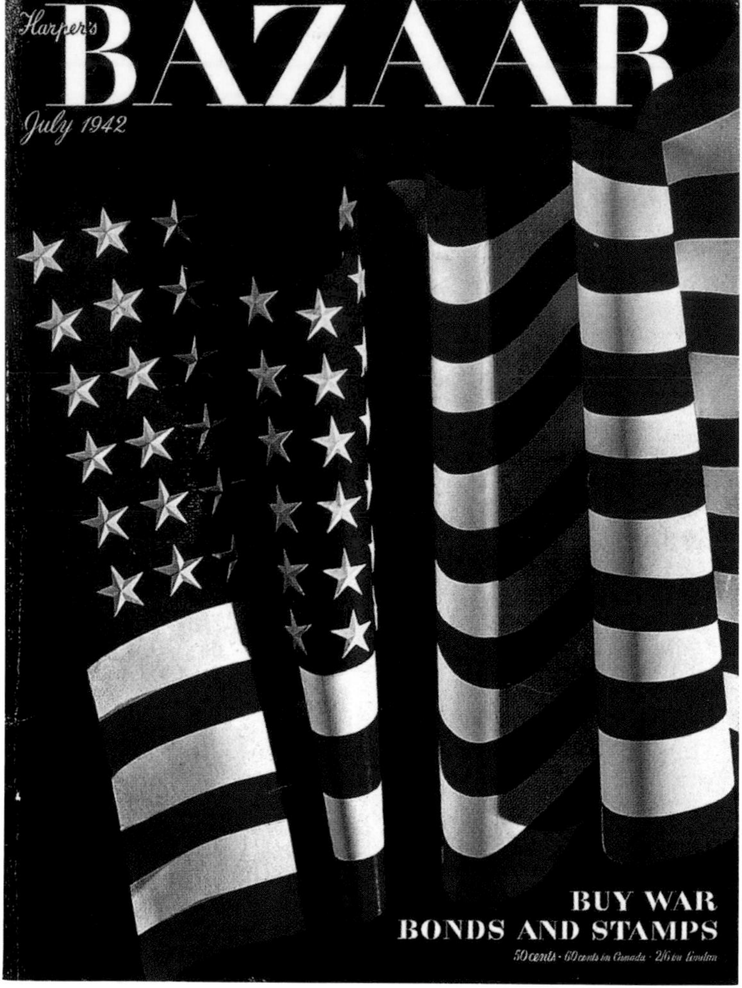

Harper's **BAZAAR**

July 1942

**BUY WAR
BONDS AND STAMPS**

50 cents · 60 cents in Canada · 2/6 in London

When Freedom from her mountain-height
Unfurled her standard to the air,
She tore the azure robe of night,
And set the stars of glory there.

★

"THE AMERICA FLAG"
Joseph Rodman Drake

Newsweek

JULY 6, 1942   15c

THE MAGAZINE OF NEWS SIGNIFICANCE

UNITED WE STAND

Buy WAR BONDS AND STAMPS FOR VICTORY

TIME

THE WEEKLY NEWSMAGAZINE

Boris Artzybasheff

LAND OF THE FREE
What price freedom before the elections?
(U. S. at War)

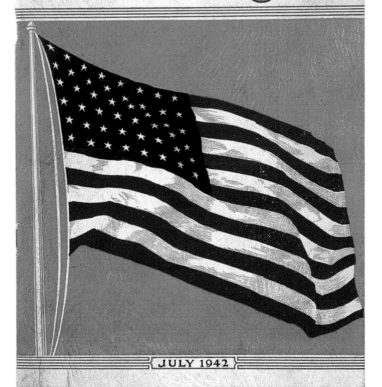

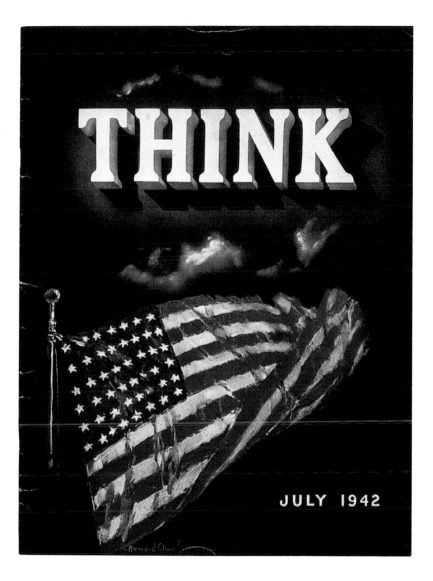

THINK

JULY 1942

JULY, 1945 · · · · · · PRICE 35 CENTS

PHOTOGRAPHED
IN AUSTRALIA
EXCLUSIVELY
FOR COLLIER'S

THE

Elks MAGAZINE

JULY 1942
20 CENTS PER COPY

42

INFANTRY JOURNAL

July, 1942   License No. TEC W-298   *Price 35¢*

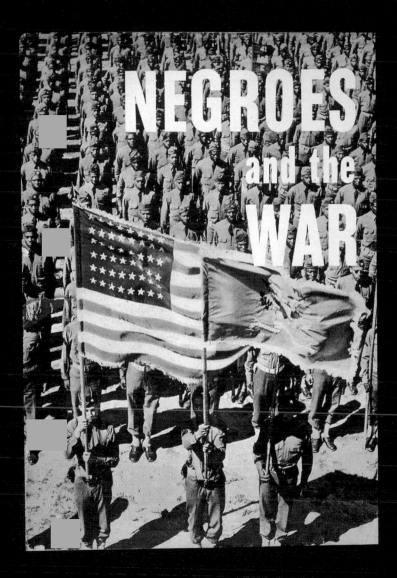

NEGROES
and the
WAR

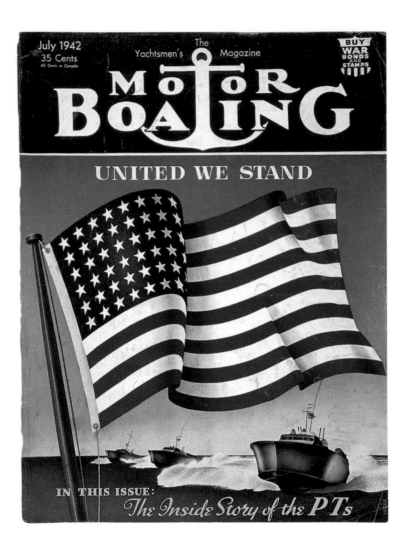

O say can you see,
by the dawn's early light,
What so proudly we hail'd at
the twilight's last gleaming,
Whose broad stripes and bright stars,
through the perilous fight
O'er the ramparts we watch'd were
so gallantly streaming?
And the rocket's red glare,
the bombs bursting in air,
Gave proof through the night that
our flag was still there,
O say does that star-spangled banner yet wave
O'er the land of the free and
the home of the brave?

★

"THE STAR SPANGLED BANNER"

Francis Scott Key

FLYING ACES

FACT
MODEL
BUILDING
FICTION

15¢

AUGUST

COMING—250,000-POUND FLYING BOATS!
by GLENN L. MARTIN

UNITED WE STAND!

"BOEING'S GO-ROUND HOUSE" • "SO YOU WANT TO BE A DIVE-BOMBER PILOT!"
MODEL SECTION: "GULL-WING GASSY" • THREE-VIEWS • "MUSTANG SOLID-SCALE"

THE RUDDER

The Magazine for Yachtsmen

"UNITED WE STAND"
BUY U. S. WAR SAVINGS BONDS AND STAMPS

July 1942
Price 35c.

Gourmet

THE MAGAZINE OF GOOD LIVING

"UNITED WE STAND"   JULY 1942 • TWENTY-FIVE CENTS

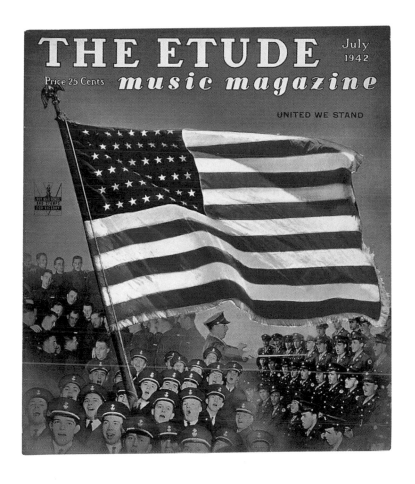

READING AT ITS BEST

THE MAGAZINE
Encore

A CONTINUING ANTHOLOGY

DENT SMITH, Editor

E. B. White · Glen H. Mullin · H. L. Mencken · John Dos Passos · Sir James H. Jeans · Nathaniel Hawthorne · Jack London · Vachel Lindsay · Voltaire · Frank Moore Colby · Sir Richard F. Burton · Edgar Evertson Saltus · Captain John Smith · Thucydides · Henry Thomas Buckle · William Graham Sumner · John Muir · Charles Darwin and others.

NOTHING CONDENSED OR SYNOPSIZED

JULY 1942   ★   25 CENTS

Who's Going to be Drafted?

July

Harpers
MAGAZINE

HARPER & BROTHERS, PUBLISHERS

Sky Trucks Coming

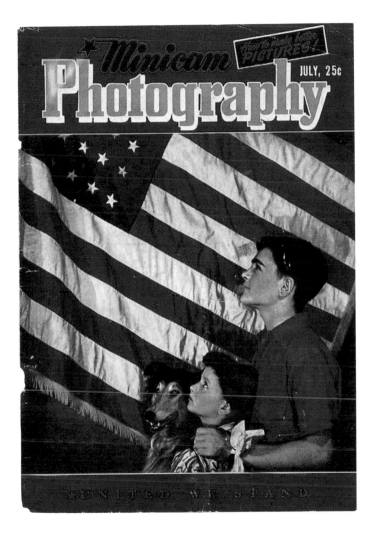

55

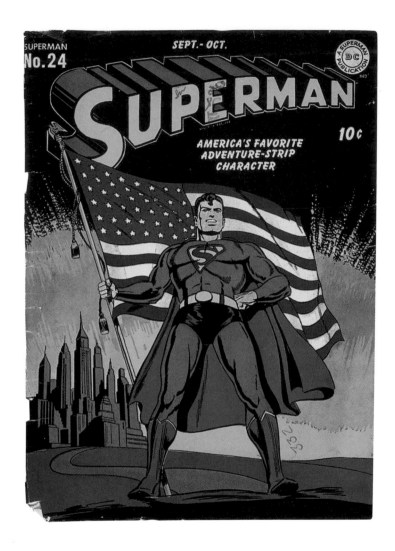

"UNITED WE STAND"

JULY 1942

BUY WAR STAMPS AND BONDS
Good News From Uncle Sam
For All Quiz Kids Club Members
See Pages 12 and 13

Brand New COMIC!
DAN'L FLANNEL
PLUS **DICK COLE** ★ **EDISON BELL** ★ **CADET**

SUMMER ISSUE 10¢

4 MOST

"What so proudly we hail..."
as
United We Stand!

Buy
WAR BONDS AND STAMPS
FOR VICTORY

Vol. 1 No. 3

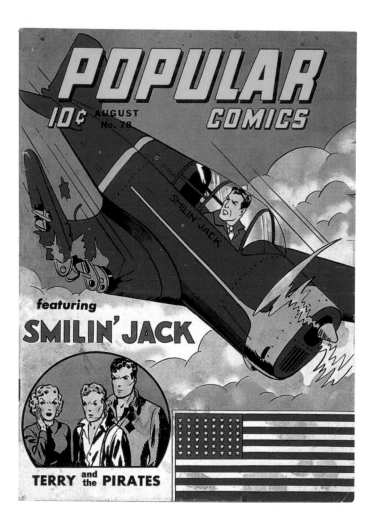

64

Scouting

JULY · 1942

HARRIS-EWING NEWS PHOTO

TREASURE HUNT for RUBBER CONTINUES—Pages 2-5
Scouts requested to continue collection of rubber as a long-term project
Also in this issue: Air Scouting — Program Ideas — War Service Notes

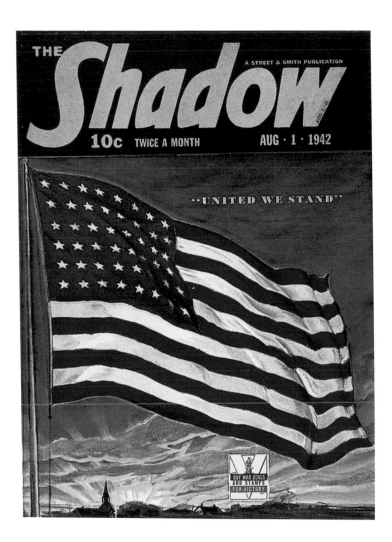

You're a grand old flag,
You're a high-flying flag
and forever in Peace may you wave.

★

"YOU'RE A GRAND OLD FLAG"
George M. Cohan

72

GM GENERAL MOTORS

PRODUCING MORE FOR VICTORY

Folks

"UNITED WE STAND"

JULY, 1942
VOL. 5   NO. 7

Dayton Presents Arms for Victory
Pageant "Plowshares"...Pages 2-5

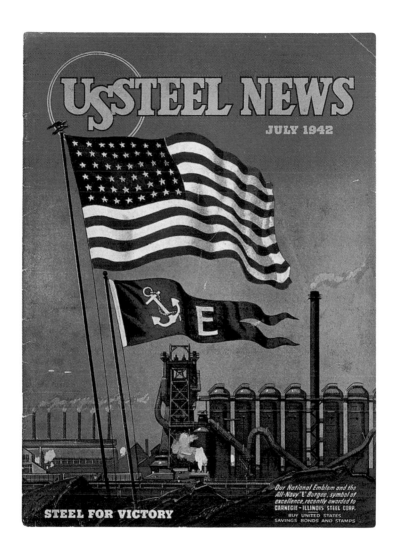

the **Beech Log**

OFFICIAL EMPLOYEES PUBLICATION OF THE BEECH AIRCRAFT CORPORATION

VOL. II   JULY 3, 1942   NO. 18

" . . . *what so*
proudly we hailed"

76

Boeing

NEWS

JULY 1942

FIREWORKS

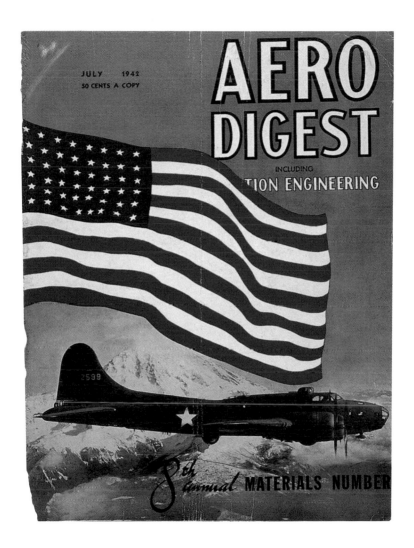

JULY 1942
50 CENTS A COPY

AERO DIGEST

INCLUDING

TION ENGINEERING

8th Annual **MATERIALS NUMBER**

THE MARTIN STAR

VOL. I   JULY 1942   NO. 6

NORTHWESTERN BELL

July · 1942

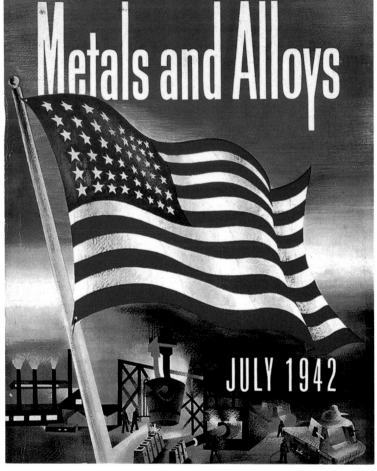

The Merck Report

Published in the Interests of Pharmacy and Medicine

JULY · 1942

LINENS &
DOMESTICS
JULY ★ NINETEEN ★ FORTY ★ TWO

I ★ PLEDGE ★ ALLEGIANCE ★ TO ★ THE ★ FLAG
OF ★ THE ★ UNITED ★ STATES ★ OF ★ AMERICA
AND ★ THE ★ REPUBLIC ★ FOR ★ WHICH ★ IT
STANDS ★ ONE ★ NATION ★ INDIVISIBLE
WITH ★ LIBERTY ★ AND ★ JUSTICE ★ FOR ★ ALL

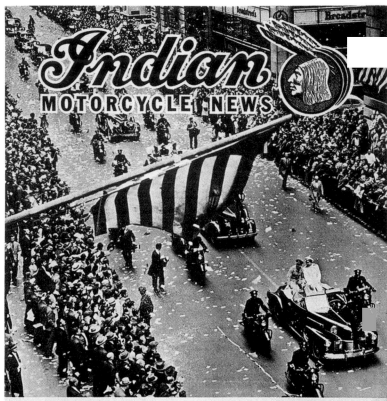

88

INTERNATIONAL NEWS PHOTO

Hail our Heroes! — A genuine New York reception once again. Up Broadway, from the Battery to City Hall, ride 15 heroes of Pearl Harbor, the Java Sea, Bataan, Corregidor and Libya escorted by a squad of New York's "finest" on Indian Police motorcycles.

AUGUST - SEPTEMBER

VOL. IX 1942 NO. VI

PUBLISHED BY THE INDIAN MOTOCYCLE CO., SPRINGFIELD, MASS., U. S. A.

HYGEIA

IN THIS ISSUE

WARTIME NEUROSES

by Walter Freeman, M.D.

Also articles on Swimming, Sunburn,
Diabetes, Home Nursing and Nutrition

JULY • 1942 • 25c

The Health Magazine of the American Medical Association

Alloys for the Allies

POPULAR MECHANICS

MAGAZINE

WRITTEN SO YOU CAN UNDERSTAND IT

AUG.
25 CENTS
30 c IN CANADA

BUY UNITED STATES
WAR SAVINGS
BONDS AND STAMPS

"UNITED WE STAND"

91

Hats off!
Along the street there comes
A blare of bugles, a ruffle of drums,
A flash of color beneath the sky:
Hats off!
The flag is passing by!

★

"THE FLAG GOES BY"
Henry Holcomb Bennett

JULY, 1942

MODERN *Beauty* SHOP

"UNITED WE STAND"

DOUBLE NUMBER

IN TWO SECTIONS

THIS SECTION	SECTION TWO
Your Professional Shop Journal	Beauty Fashions for Your Patrons

WHAT HAPPENS TO YOUR AMMUNITION TAX? by HAROLD TITUS

Field & Stream

BUY UNITED STATES
WAR SAVINGS
BONDS AND STAMPS

"UNITED WE STAND"

July 1942

15¢

IN CANADA 20c

Country Gentleman

JULY, 1942

BUY WAR SAVINGS
BONDS AND STAMPS

In This Issue: FARMERS IN THE WAR FACTORY, By Arthur W. Baum
Featured in Country Gentlewoman: A GAY FOOD CHART FOR YOUR KITCHEN

AMERICAN FORESTS

JULY 1942

FLOWER GROWER

The Home Gardener's Magazine

BUY WAR BONDS
AND STAMPS
FOR VICTORY

"United We Stand"

JULY 1942   25 CENTS

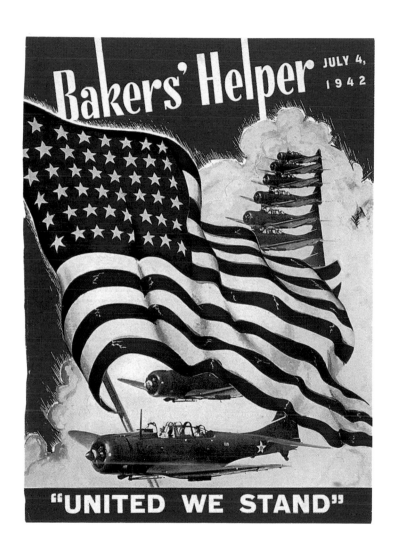

July 1942 10¢

Successful Farming

The Magazine of Farm Business and Farm Homes

★AGRICULTURE IS
FUNDAMENTAL

A FARMER PLANS FOR TODAY AND TOMORROW—SEE PAGE 11

Better Homes & Gardens

MORE THAN 2,400,000 CIRCULATION

JULY 1942 15¢

★ Home is the Strength of the Nation

PLANNING FOR TODAY AND TOMORROW—Page 18

SUMMER COOK BOOK – Frosty drinks • Steps to canning • Meals-in-a-basket • and more

My country, 'tis of Thee,
Sweet Land of Liberty
Of thee I sing;
Land where my fathers died,
Land of the pilgrims' pride,
From every mountain side
Let Freedom ring.

★

Grand birthright of our sires,
Our altars and our fires
Keep we still pure!
Our starry flag unfurled,
The hope of all the world,
In peace and light impearled,
God hold secure!

★

"AMERICA"
Samuel F. Smith

FARM
JOURNAL
AND *Farmer's Wife*

July 1942
5¢

BUY WAR
BONDS AND
STAMPS

"United We Stand"

July, 1942

Capper's Farmer

THE MAGAZINE OF IDEAS FOR PRACTICAL FARMERS

ELIZABETH CUTLER

THE LICKIN' THAT DOESN'T HURT

BUY U. S. WAR SAVINGS BONDS
AND STAMPS

The Magazine

ANTIQUES

JULY 1 9 4 2

50 CENTS

The New
PENCIL
POINTS
JULY · 1942

NATIONAL

AUDITGRAM

Published by the National Association of Bank Auditors and Comptrollers

Volume XXIII   MAY • 1952   Number 5

THE AMERICAN'S CREED

"I believe in the United States of America as a government of the people, by the people, for the people; whose just powers are derived from the consent of the governed; a democracy in a Republic; a sovereign Nation of many sovereign States; a perfect Union, one and inseparable; established upon these principles of freedom, equality, justice and humanity for which American patriots sacrificed their lives and fortunes.

"I therefore believe it is my duty to my country to love it; to support its Constitution; to obey its laws; to respect its flag; and to defend it against all enemies."

"THE BETTER THE AUDITOR, THE SAFER THE BANK"

THE ARCHITECTURAL
FORUM

JULY 1942

Edward Steichen and Carl Sandburg's ROAD TO VICTORY

W-N-Y-F

With New York Firemen

Photo by Raymond Holzriegel

JULY 1942

Symbolic of the Fire Department's essential role in the wartime protection of New York City and its harbor is this view of the "Fire Fighter's" flag saluted to a brisk breeze. Seen far down in sharp battle relife, ready to defend bravely and the liberty for which she stands.

Index of Magazines

McCALL'S

THREE MAGAZINES IN ONE

Our Biggest July Fiction Issue

RUTH LYONS • BARBARA ALDRICH • FAITH BALDWIN

ELIZABETH GREGG PATTERSON • ELIZABETH SEIFERT

JULY 1942

FIFTEEN CENTS